Home Front
Christmas

IDEAS AND INSPIRATION FROM

JOCASTA INNES ✫ ANNE MCKEVITT
STEWART & SALLY WALTON ✫ KEVIN MCCLOUD

TEXT BY JUDY SPOURS

PHOTOGRAPHS BY PAUL BRICKNELL AND MARK GATEHOUSE

BBC Books

This book is published to accompany the
BBC Television series *Home Front*
Editor Daisy Goodwin

Published by BBC Books
an imprint of BBC Worldwide Limited,
Woodlands, 80 Wood Lane,
London W12 0TT

First published 1997
Written and compiled by Judy Spours

© BBC Worldwide Limited

Designs © Jocasta Innes, Kevin McCloud, Anne McKevitt
and Stewart & Sally Walton 1997

ISBN 0 563 38377 1

Designed by Janet James
Photography by Paul Bricknell and Mark Gatehouse
Stylist: Sue Russell

Printed and bound in Great Britain by Butler & Tanner Ltd, Frome and London
Colour separations by Radstock Reproductions Ltd, Midsomer Norton

Cover printed by Belmont Press Ltd, Northampton

Contents

Introduction 4

JOCASTA INNES
A Traditional Christmas 8
Shooting Star
A Print Room
Bagging Up
An Edible Tree

ANNE McKEVITT
Christmas Present and Future 22
A Wreath for the 90s
A Light Meal
The Fireside
Co-ordinated Wrapping

STEWART & SALLY WALTON
A Family Christmas 36
Colour and Light
Norwegian Wood
Window Stencilling
Cellophane Wrapping

KEVIN McCLOUD
A Medieval Feast 50
Shades of Green
The Bedecked Chandelier
Gilded Nature
A Treasure Chest

Acknowledgements and Useful Addresses 64

Introduction

The essence of the Christmas spirit has to be entertainment – of children
with games and presents and the excitement of it all, and of friends and
family, who we welcome into our homes at this time of year more than at
any other. The way in which we decorate our houses for the season is
therefore very important to us. We want the tree to look enticing, we
choose rich colours to add warmth, and we make sure the lighting is
mellow enough to put everyone at their ease. We even want the front door
to appear inviting. Above all, we want a touch of magic in the way it all
looks, something that represents our own particular Christmas sparkle.

Home Front designers Jocasta Innes, Anne McKevitt, Kevin McCloud
and Stewart and Sally Walton are no exception to this rule. Viewers of
BBC television's series will have seen them at work on many and ingenious

permanent decorating projects, but in this book
they turn their imaginations to the more temporary
arrangements they make for Christmas. Yet they
give Christmas decoration the same energy,
invention and daring as they usually lend to more
serious schemes.

Here, they are perhaps more conscious than
ever of keeping costs low and of using materials
which are easy to find, while still creating decorations which are beautiful
to look at. All four designers have exploited nature to the full, either by
combing the countryside for holly and ivy or pine cones, or by raiding the
kitchen cupboard for groceries which will look wonderful and smell great.
All, too, have invented projects which are original and attractive, but
which are also really achievable by the amateur following the pictures and
instructions given in the book.

Beyond this, the four designers' plans for Christmas are very different, as we have come to expect from seeing their work on television. As a result, this little book contains an enormous range of Christmas ideas, for the inside and outside of the house, for packing presents and for setting tables and to suit very varied tastes. Whether you want to stick with the traditional or branch out into a very modern Christmas look, and whether you have a period house or a contemporary flat, you are likely to find something here to suit. And, in any case, you won't need a bottomless purse or an addiction to department stores to follow the inspiration our designers give – you will be able to bring together their ideas cheaply and easily.

Kevin McCloud relies almost totally on winter foliage – found free if you live in the countryside and at comparatively little cost in town – for his designs. Stewart and Sally Walton show how you can mix Christmas motifs from a range of cultures, adapting what you already have on hand at home to fit the bill. Anne McKevitt approaches Christmas with no preconceptions, offering the shock of the new for very little outlay. And Jocasta Innes stays traditional, but gives convention a new edge, making elegant arrangements from the most basic ingredients. To complete the picture of these very personal styles, the four Christmas design schemes have been done in the designers' houses, giving us a fascinating glimpse into their own Home Fronts.

A Regency house in the heart of London's Spitalfields, with a fabulous staircase, is a setting to which a traditional Christmas comes easy. The backdrop is in place, and needs only the smallest elaboration.

A traditional Christmas

Jocasta Innes's Christmas may be elegant, naturally enough, but it is also earthy: her overriding interest is in the food. On Christmas Eve she hosts a big family party, a strictly adult affair. Champagne corks pop, and a toast is glugged from her partner's precious Venetian glasses which, she says, is like drinking out of bird baths.

The food strays from the straight and narrow into a cuisine Jocasta describes as 'chic peasant' – smoked salmon is followed by venison or pheasant and as none of her family likes Christmas pudding it may be substituted with a Sussex Pond pudding – made with suet – or a partly-cooked, gooey chocolate mousse. Although the food is a little alternative, Jocasta's decorations are time-honoured and traditional.

Christmas Day is a confusion of presents, which she loves to make and give, gauging their popularity by the degree to which she is reluctant to part with them. She lights the fire in the living room and someone else opens the window, children dash around excitedly, and so the day goes on. The company finally settles to watch films on TV – you know the ones!

ABOVE: CAROL SINGERS' LANTERNS
AND SUSTAINING MINCE PIES WAIT
FOR ACTION ON JOCASTA'S DOORSTEP.
LEFT: LONG FRONDS OF IVY ARE USED
TO DECORATE THE CURVING HANDRAIL
OF THE STAIRCASE. SIMPLY WRAP IT
AROUND, SECURING HERE AND THERE
WITH FLORIST'S WIRE, UNTIL IT LOOKS
VERDANT ENOUGH, BUSHY EVEN.

Shooting star

There is no denying that punching tin is hard work, but it is perfectly feasible for the amateur, and the finished star will last forever. Jocasta started with just one, large star, but got carried away: the addition of the smaller star, spaced with the cork, gave the whole piece an extra dimension which was well worth the extra work. The baubles are an optional extra – you could leave them out for a minimal look, or substitute coloured ones, or beads, for a glamorous model.

YOU WILL NEED... *Pencil, paper and ruler • Tin sheet to accommodate your size of stars • 'Snips' scissors for cutting metal • Block of scrap wood • Screwdriver • Large nail • Hammer • Cork from a wine bottle • Silver craft paint • Paintbrush • Glue gun • Frosted silver tree baubles*

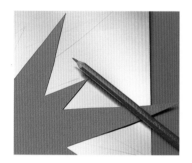

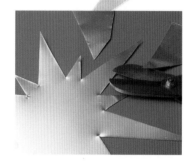

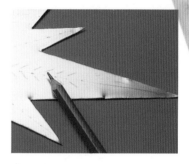

1 *Using a ruler, pencil and paper draw two corresponding star shapes, one about twice the size of the other, and cut them out to make templates. Jocasta drew quite an elaborate star, but a simpler shape would still be effective. Place the templates onto the sheet metal and draw around them.*

2 *Using 'snips' metal-cutting scissors, cut around the outside of the star shapes. Work from the circumference inwards to make the job easier and to form sharp points and clean edges.*

3 *Mark up the cut-out tin stars in pencil with guidelines and notches where you want to decorate them with punched holes. This is important, as if you punch a hole in the wrong place, there is nothing you can do to disguise it.*

4 Lay the star on the block of wood and punch holes in with the sharp end of a screwdriver and with a large nail, tapping them through with a hammer. The hole punching does require patience and care.

5 Cut a 2.5 cm (1 in) piece from a cork and paint the edge with silver craft paint. Using strong adhesive, stick the cork to the centre of the large star, and then fix the smaller star on the top.

6 Remove the hanging loops from the tree baubles, then glue them into an arrangement at the centre of the star. A final, larger and centrally placed bauble covers up all the blobs of glue underneath.

This is the most elegant of solutions to the problem of how on earth you display all those Christmas cards. For a few seasonal weeks, it almost looks as though Jocasta's house has been redecorated specially for Christmas, with the cards hung on the walls alongside the paintings.

A *Print* Room

During the eighteenth century, and amongst a certain class – particularly of those gentlemen who had gone on Grand Tours around the architectural splendours of Europe – there grew a mania for collecting prints. A similar problem occurred then as we now have with Christmas cards – how and where to display such large collections to best effect? A fashion for 'print rooms' developed, in which the walls would be covered with prints – variously framed and decoratively linked with swags and bows. The print room was a curiosity, shown off to visitors as testament to the travels and taste of its owner.

This idea has been reproduced as part of interior decoration schemes in the late twentieth century and it can also be easily copied on a temporary basis for Christmas cards, stuck onto the wall with photocopied bows and motifs in between. Jocasta has decorated her hallway, but the print room technique could be extended throughout the house. Perhaps children would like to have their cards in their own rooms, maybe linked together with less authentic-looking but brighter bows and ribbons. It does help to have the backdrop of a period house, but there is no reason why the idea should not translate to all sorts of interiors.

ABOVE: SUN, MOON AND STARS GREET VISITORS ON THE STAIR WALL; RIGHT: THE SWEEP OF THE STAIRCASE REFLECTS IN A HUGE WALL MIRROR, THE PERFECT SETTING FOR A BORDER OF CARDS; FAR RIGHT: THE TEMPORARY PRINT ROOM ARRANGEMENT OF CARDS AROUND THE CURVING HALLWAY BLENDS WITH THE REAL PRINTS AND PAINTINGS ON THE WALL BEYOND.

Framing the cards

Jocasta bought a couple of sheets of printed classical swags, ribbons, knots and monstrous-looking creatures from a National Trust shop, and had them enlarged to a size suitable for the hallway walls.

The secret of a good print room effect is to start by building up a framework of the photocopied motifs into which the cards can fit. Mirrors can be bordered, with swags above – doing this over the fireplace looks especially good – and large wall areas can be pasted with long parallel strips ending with tassels, like towering bell-pulls.

YOU WILL NEED... *Christmas cards • Enlarged sheets of swags, ribbons and bows • Sharp scissors • Low-tack spray adhesive, Blu-Tack or double-sided tape*

You need to use an adhesive which will not fix the cards permanently and which will not mark the paintwork or wallpaper. Jocasta used a low-tack spray adhesive, applying a very fine coat, just enough to hold the cards in place. Blu-Tack or double-sided tape are possibilities, and are useful for sticking the cards closed so that they don't swing open unattractively once in place.

HIGH-UP AREAS OF WALL SPACE – OFTEN USUALLY LEFT BLANK – SHOULD NOT BE IGNORED, PARTICULARLY IF YOU HAVE SCORES OF CARDS TO ACCOMMODATE.

Bagging Up

Despite her previous New Year's resolution, Jocasta always leaves the provision of paper, string, ribbon and tags to the last minute, literally, and is caught red-handed by her family as she tries to bundle up a mountain of presents at the eleventh hour. This year she is forearmed. Brightly-coloured fabric bags, of all shapes and sizes, can accommodate even the most awkwardly-shaped presents, and will save time on Christmas Eve.

Most of these bags are decorated with rubber stamp motifs, but other methods are equally attractive: you could roughly machine

on contrasting cut-outs of fabric; or make a stencil of a star, spray glue through it onto the bags and then attach glitter with a brush; or glue on sequins at random or in a pattern.

ABOVE RIGHT: CHAMPAGNE AND WINE IN ONLY PARTIAL DISGUISE, BUT MADE SUMPTUOUS WITH A GOLD LAUREL LEAF TAG AND RIBBONS; BELOW RIGHT: VARIOUS RUBBER-STAMPED MOTIFS ON BAGS OF ALL SHAPES AND SIZES.

Present bags

Felt has long been available in vibrant colours, and hessian is now also made in delicious hues, subtler than those of felt because of the dark, natural colour of the material. Felt doesn't fray, which means that you don't have to worry about making pukka hems – a quick zoom round with the sewing machine is all that's needed. Hessian does fray, so either cut with pinking shears or turn over the top edge to the inside.

YOU WILL NEED...
Brightly coloured felt • Coloured hessian • Scissors • Pinking shears • Sewing machine and cottons • Rubber stamps – here in star, flower and pear shapes • Stencil paints in silver, gold and colours • Small artist's brush • Laurel or other evergreen leaves • Silver and/or gold spray paint • Raffia • Black marker pen

1 *Using scissors and pinking shears, cut out squares and rectangles of felt and hessian in different sizes to make a variety of bags. Bags can be one colour, or have contrasting colours on either side.*

2 *Machine three sides of each bag. Those cut with pinking shears from felt can be left as they are, but turn the others inside out to hide the stitching, and perhaps turn down an edge at the top.*

3 *Colour up the rubber stamps with a generous coating of stencil paint – gold, silver or another shade – using a small artist's brush.*

4 *Press the stamps down firmly onto the bags to make a strong image, or more lightly to produce a vaguer effect. The stamping does not have to be perfect.*

5 *Using newspaper as a backing, spray paint laurel or other large evergreen leaves in gold or silver, making sure you give them a thick coat. Allow to dry, then write on them.*

6 *Bag your presents and tie the tops with bunched-up lengths of raffia. Write your greetings on the leaves with marker pen, and slip the stems under the tied raffia.*

Christmas styling is all that much easier
if you have a beautifully curtained upstairs window
like this one in which to show off the tree.
As luck, rather than actual seasonal
design, would have it, the
light fitting on this landing
is in the shape of a star.

An Edible Tree

Everything about this tree (except for the tin star at the top) is either edible or spicy. The plant itself is a handsome bay, which has been pruned to a perfect conical shape. Bay trees are expensive, but can be a very versatile investment. The leaves can be used for cooking all year long; the tree can be put to decorative use in the garden in summer; and it will last for years and many Christmases, potted on as it grows.

The decorated tree is extraordinarily pretty, with its colours co-ordinated by nature alone. The ingredients for the decorations are inexpensive and readily available: popcorn, chilli peppers, kumquats, cloves, cinnamon sticks, striped candy sticks – nothing more. Florist's wire, strong cotton and raffia are all that are needed for threading, tying and attaching.

There are plenty of other foods which would look good, too, such as gingerbread men (gilded, angel-shaped ones would be the ultimate), cranberry or raisin strings, small red apples or crab apples; or nuts, particularly shiny cobs still on their stems. And, of course, foil-covered chocolates are always loved by children.

LEFT: THE SIMPLEST BUT MOST ELEGANT OF TREES, POSITIONED
PERFECTLY BETWEEN EXTRAVAGANT CURTAIN TIE-BACKS;
ABOVE RIGHT: TRADITIONAL RED, GREEN AND GOLD, PROVIDED BY
CHILLI PEPPER, BAY LEAVES AND KUMQUAT.

Tree treats

All the edible decorations are very easy to make, just a little time-consuming. However, making them is just the sort of project that small children love, particularly the popcorn threading, although you may have to keep a

of raffia, one formed into a loop for hanging on the tree. The kumquats are studded round with cloves in two concentric circles. A small length of florist's wire, threaded through one end of the kumquat oval, can be hooked over and attached to the bay branches.

Wrapped candy sticks in a variety of colours, much used decoratively in the U.S.A., are now easy to find over here, and give added glitz. The bonus of all these foods is that the tree will smell delicious, all fruit and spice.

watch that you do end up with chains for the tree rather than just a few full stomachs. Make a big pan of popcorn, provide needles with long, sturdy thread and ask the children to intersperse the popcorn with hanging chilli peppers, threaded through at one end.

The cinnamon sticks are just bunched up and tied roughly around with a few pieces

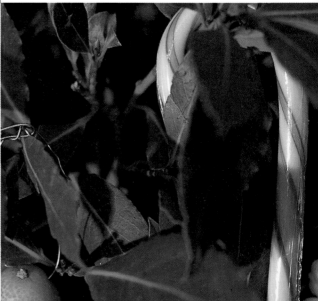

Scandinavian Lights

In Sweden every house window has its candle – a nightlight or a wick in oil – on Christmas Eve, and very pretty it looks, too.

LINED UP ALONG THE SHELF OF A LUNETTE ABOVE AN EXTERIOR DOOR, THE GLASS JARS, TWINKLING WITH JAZZY COLOUR, REALLY LOOK THE BUSINESS AND PUT ARRIVING GUESTS INTO FESTIVE MOOD.

Instead of forking out for expensive candle-holders or glass oil lights, we improvised with a selection of old glass jars and cheap tumblers. We painted them with glass/ceramic paints, of which there are a number now on the market. These come in a dazzling array of colours, and paint on easily and smoothly. Cheap white nightlights are dropped into the glasses and lit with a long taper.

Christmas *Present and* Future

Anne McKevitt sees no reason to live with the restrictions of reds and greens of Christmases past. Her light and airy magenta and turquoise designs pull Christmas decoration firmly into the 1990s.

The suggestion that we look to nothing traditonal for inspiration when designing Christmas is not just liberating, it is almost subversive. But Anne McKevitt is not a designer with a mission to shock; rather, she has a clear belief in new, fresh, innovative ideas, and a mistrust of the adage that the past was better than the present. She is as attached as most of us are to the memory of the traditional Christmases of her childhood – she just sees no good reason to imitate them now.

For Anne, Christmas is tailored down, modern and very inexpensive. It requires no gruelling trips to the packed seasonal departments of major stores. Instead, a stroll to your local hardware shop for an unprejudiced look at buckets and pan scourers, and a stop at the corner shop for some dried pasta, will be sufficient. It is all a matter of finding decorative potential where you have never looked for it before.

THE ENTRANCE TO THE HOUSE IS ELEGANT AND INVITING, A VERY SIMPLE SCHEME WHICH SUCCEEDS BY USING LOTS OF A FEW BASIC ELEMENTS TO ACHIEVE MAXIMUM IMPACT. LOW COST IS PARTICULARLY IMPORTANT TO BEAR IN MIND HERE, TOO, JUST IN CASE PARTS OF THE DESIGN SHOULD DISAPPEAR DURING THE NIGHT.

ARMFULS OF TWIGS ARE DECORATED
WITH STRINGS OF PAINTED, DRIED PENNE
PASTA AND PUSHED INTO GALVANISED
BUCKETS, WHICH CAN BE PUT TO GOOD
USE IN THE GARDEN IN THE NEW YEAR.
THE COLOURS USED HERE BY THE FRONT
DOOR HINT AT THOSE WHICH ARE TO
BE FOUND BEYOND, INSIDE THE HOUSE,
AND THE CANDLES AND LANTERNS ARE
A WELCOMING ADDITION WHEN GUESTS
ARE EXPECTED.

A wreath for the 90s

Although door wreaths are traditional, this one is brought bang up to date by its colour and humour. It is quick, easy and cheap to make and part of it, at least, is bio-degradable – the chocolate sardines will be happily disposed of by the last young guests of the season.

YOU WILL NEED... *A wire wreath frame (available from florists) • Old newspaper • Roll of fishing line or jeweller's nylon thread • Coloured tissue paper – Anne used turquoise blue • Roll of colourless cellophane • Adhesive tape • Roll of silver ribbon 1 cm wide and about 10 metres long • Foil-covered chocolate sardines (or other foil-wrapped sweets) • Small roll of very narrow silver ribbon • Length of tulle netting in the same colour as the tissue paper and a smaller strip in a contrasting colour*

1 *Scrunch up sheets of newspaper and wrap them around the wire wreath frame, bit by bit, following them with the nylon thread, twisted round and round. Finally, knot the thread to secure the newspaper.*

2 *Wind lengths of turquoise tissue paper around the newspaper base, leaving no gaps, and securing again as you go with nylon thread wound around.*

3 *Use one continuous strip from the roll of cellophane and wind it round and round over the turquoise tissue, securing the ends with adhesive tape on the underside of the wreath.*

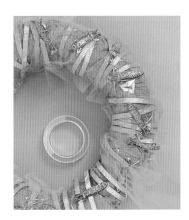

4 Wind a long piece of the silver ribbon at differing angles around the wreath, and secure with a knot on the underside. At intervals, tie on foil-covered sardines by their tails with the very narrow silver ribbon.

5 Wrap the wreath round and round with the long piece of turquoise tulle netting, and, once again, wrap around with nylon thread as you go and knot to secure it.

6 Finish by tying on a piece of contrasting-coloured tulle netting to the top. Fix the wreath to the front door with a long piece of nylon thread tied around the wreath, hung over the door and secured on the inside with drawing pins.

A Light Meal

Anne's dining-room is a refreshing experience for eyes and stomachs heavy with Christmas excess. The room has a simple exoticism, radiating out from the single pink orchid in its bowl of silver balls.

Anne has created an entire, light Christmas environment for the dining-room, free of other items or clutter, because she feels that a good design idea is hardly worth doing if it is diluted down. Here she will serve what she freely admits will be the only meal which she cooks herself from start to finish the whole year long. And even the food will be a break with tradition, a vegetarian Christmas meal.

Turquoise and magenta – a sort of up-beat, contemporary version of green and red – are exploited to the full in this room scheme, toned with fresh foliage greens, copper and silver. The frosted silver balls hung by threads from the ceiling give an ethereal, space age feel, and the pale blue walls are a calming backdrop. Champagne is ready in the ice bucket and friends and family are the essential missing ingredient that will enter later into her alternative Christmas design.

The table setting

The table setting shows a studied attention to detail – from the toning bowls of rose and pistachio Turkish delight to the candles floating in water coloured with very diluted clothes' dye. Again, the emphasis is on creating style from inexpensive, readily available materials. The tablecloth base is a king-size cream bed sheet, overlaid with strips of turquoise cotton dress fabric, bought for a couple of pounds a metre. Narrower strips of the turquoise tulle netting that was also used for the wreath are then laid over the top. The tableware is kept as simple as possible, so that it doesn't fight with other elements of the design – plain glass, white china, silver cutlery.

OPPOSITE, ABOVE LEFT: CASTOR OIL LEAVES, SPRAY-PAINTED SILVER, ARE ATTACHED TO THE BACKS OF THE CHAIRS WITH SILVER-SPRAYED CLOTHES' PEGS; ABOVE RIGHT: THE CENTREPIECE ORCHID BOWL IS CHEAP PLASTIC DECORATED WITH TORN, COLOURED TISSUE PAPER, STUCK ON WITH PVA GLUE; SIMPLE, WHITE CHURCH CANDLES ARE DECORATED WITH GLUED-ON GLASS CABOCHONS; BELOW LEFT: NAPKINS ARE INEXPENSIVE, UNHEMMED PIECES OF DRESS FABRIC, THREADED THROUGH PLASTIC BANGLES; BELOW RIGHT: THE WALL DECORATION IS CONSTRUCTED FROM FERN LEAVES – LEFT GREEN OR SPRAY PAINTED SILVER OR COPPER – FIXED HAPHAZARDLY TO A FLORIST'S WIRE FRAME AND ATTACHED TO THE WALL WITH A PICTURE HOOK.

The Fireside

Over-designed schemes and clutter do not appeal to Anne at all. The fireside shows both her love of experimentation and her desire to sweep away decorations of the past. It is amazing to see what can be done with a few galvanised buckets, some pan scourers, garden tags and a bag or two of pasta when they are put in the right hands. Although the arrangements are stylised compared to those on other Christmas hearth-

sides, they are colourful and full of fun. A roaring fire and generous plate of candles sunk into sand lend warmth, and the up-lighters on the wall provide an added glow of light.

Spiral tree

Anne's Christmas tree is pared down to its bare, skeletal essentials of form and shape. Even the fairy on the top is there, literally, in name only. This synthetic tree is far more exciting and appealing than bought ones which pretend too hard to be the real thing. After Christmas, the spiral can be flat packed to store and you could easily re-paint it in different colours to fit in with another new decorative plan.

1 Find the centre of the square of cardboard by drawing feint diagonals from corner to corner with a pencil and ruler. Tie a pencil to a long piece of string. Fix the string a short length from the pencil to the centre point of the card with a drawing pin. Draw a circle. Remove the pin, lengthen the string by 15 cm (6 in) and repeat the process, drawing five or more concentric circles.

2 Working onto a cutting mat or board, cut out the middle circle with the scalpel. Then cut out the series of hoops, keeping to the pencil lines.

3 Spray paint or paint half of the hoops in turquoise and the other half in magenta, colouring both sides of the cardboard. (Make sure to wear a face mask and have doors and windows open for ventilation.)

YOU WILL NEED... *Large square of brown cardboard • Pencil • String • Drawing pin • Ruler • Cutting mat or board • Scalpel and spare blades • Matt emulsion or spray paint in turquoise and magenta • Roll of fishing line or jeweller's nylon thread • Large nail • Marker pen • Scouring pads, plastic cutlery and copper plant tags as decorations*

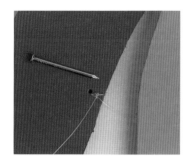

4 Mark out four holes on each hoop at regular intervals around the inside circumference, about a centimetre from the edge. Push through a large nail to make holes. Make four holes around the circumference of the solid middle circle. Starting with this circle (the apex of the tree), link the hoops on lengths of nylon string, tying it through the nail holes. Here, the hoops of the tree are about 25 cm (10 in) apart.

5 Cut an arc shape from a cardboard off-cut, spray paint or paint it turquoise, and write 'FAIRY' with marker pen. Attach four nylon strings from the holes in the circular top section, tie together and fix the tree to the ceiling with drawing pins. The tree should suspend down, clear of the floor. Slot the fairy card into the strings at the top.

6 Now decorate your tree. Thread nylon through the copper scouring pads and the copper garden tags and tie nylon threads around the items of plastic cutlery. Make nail holes in the hoops of the tree at random and tie on the decorations, hanging them down by their nylon threads.

The mantel

Nothing could be simpler to create than this arrangement for a modern mantel. The painted pasta, scourers and garden tags can be strung like beads onto nylon threads of varying lengths and attached at the sides of the mantel shelf with adhesive tape or drawing pins. Cut the holographic paper into curly S-shapes with a small hole at the

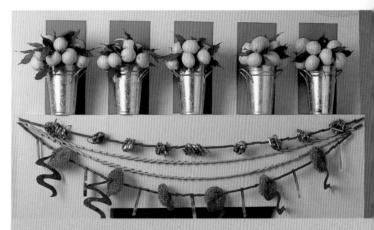

YOU WILL NEED... Dried pasta – tagliatelle portions painted copper; penne painted turquoise and magenta • Nylon thread, as before • Copper scouring pads • Copper garden tags • Adhesive tape • Magenta holographic paper • Galvanised buckets • Oasis • Florist's wire • Lemons • Leaves • Blu-Tack

top for threading. Fill the galvanised buckets with florist's oasis, then push florist's wire through one end of each lemon, loop it round and twist it into a stem, which can then be pushed into the oasis. Use evergreen leaves to garnish the lemons – even holly would be permissible here. To add a finishing background touch, fix rectangles of turquoise paper to the wall behind the buckets with Blu-Tack.

The packaging of these presents is an ideal camouflage to the identity of their contents, some even appearing to masquerade as small, furry animals.

Co-ordinated Wrapping

The overall colour scheme of Anne's Christmas is entertainingly carried through to the wrapping of her presents, which she designs into one-colour, multi-textured groups. She does admit that some friends are embarrassed by their own inferior wrapping skills, and that she has even been known to relegate gifts with dodgy paper designs to a cupboard so that they don't mar the look of her room.

The desire to have these colourful piles of highly-designed presents under the tree comes from Anne's childhood. Then, it seemed the Christmas tree was always too small to

surround with presents, and was disappointingly perched up on a dresser. She always longed to have piles of presents, beautifully wrapped and cunningly disguised, heaped around the tree, and loves to create them now.

Anne became an obsessive present packer as a small child, and is now so adept that some of her friends refuse to spoil her wrappings by opening their gifts. She is trying to encourage them to do so by using cheaper and cheaper materials, but the effects are still unique and must be difficult to rip apart without a second glance.

The materials Anne used to wrap the presents include coloured tissue paper, painted corrugated cardboard, coloured cellophane, tulle netting, builders' scrim, painted pasta, fun fur, textured fabric and ribbons. The labels are, again, copper garden tags. The only wrapping rule is to be as inventive and playful as you can.

STEWART &
SALLY WALTON

A *family* Christmas

On Christmas Eve, members of an extended family make their various ways to a bright, welcoming Victorian house overlooking the sea. They are an essential ingredient of what Stewart and Sally Walton disarmingly call their 'jumble sale of a designer Christmas'.

Dinner is on Christmas Eve night, with everyone dressed-up to the nines, including the children, who love the formality – the boys have even been known to struggle into out-sized suits for the occasion. The whole family cram around an elaborately decorated table, lit by candles, while nightlights flicker everywhere at the windows.

Christmas Day itself is for presents, and there are always spare packages under the tree for unexpected guests. A walk on the beach, a board game or two and a drink to friends absent and present all make for a relaxing time. The house itself glitters, inside and out, with the light and colour of decorations old and new, traditional and decidedly off-beat.

RIGHT: RUDOLFO THE MEXICAN REINDEER IS MADE FROM A WOVEN SPANISH DONKEY HEAD – A HOLIDAY RELIC – ATTACHED WITH FLORIST'S WIRE TO A WILLOW WREATH. HIS ANTLERS ARE GOLD-SPRAYED TWIGS AND HIS FIESTA-STYLE DECORATIONS ARE FLUORESCENT AND GLITTERY POM-POMS, PLASTIC FRUIT AND ARTIFICIAL ANEMONES, STUCK ON WITH BLOBS OF GLUE.

A mix of styles – Mexican, jungle, home-grown traditional – combine in a riot of colour in the living-room, and are mellowed by soft lighting.

Colour and Light

Stewart and Sally's son Sam, a designer in his own right, had the idea for the fairy lights in goldfish bowls and glass vases which are central to the living-room's Christmas design. They make a magical waterfall of light, and four or five bowls, together with the coal fire and the tree lights,

are enough to illuminate the whole room. Fairy lights require very low voltage and are therefore safe to use with children.

Coloured lights work equally well, perhaps even trailing over the edges of bowls, but white was chosen here as there is so much colour elsewhere in the room. The effect is of carnival fun, but with cards displayed all over the place and sheep still abiding by the fire, the Waltons' fiesta theme mingles perfectly with more conventional elements of Christmas.

The Waltons' Christmas tree goes up on the 23rd of December and is designed by committee – the whole family have a go.

Norwegian Wood

This is the traditional tree we all know and love, a cone-shaped spruce with all its associations of childhood, Scandinavia and of Christmas lights in Trafalgar Square. It probably also reminds us, as it does the Waltons, of the seasonal argument of how to get the thing to stand up straight! Here the terracotta pot is weighted with gravel from the garden and the tree is wedged in, using bricks.

The decorations are all hand-made by adults and children alike. The family have been making decorations for twenty years, and usually something to represent each year's design theme is hung on the tree. The children decorate up to their own heights and later, after bedtime, the adults continue the design to the top. A Mexican tin angel, decorated with jewels and pom-poms, highlights the carnival feel of of the room.

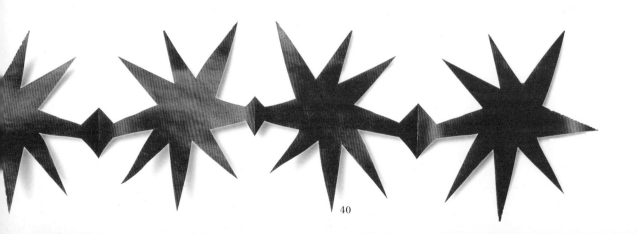

PAPER CHAINS SOMEHOW ENCAPSULATE
ALL THE EXCITEMENT OF A CHILD'S
CHRISTMAS: ALL THAT SNIPPING AND
FINGER-CROSSING IN THE HOPE OF
PRODUCING A WADGE OF PAPER THAT
PULLS OUT INTO SOMETHING LONG,
SCULPTED AND ALTOGETHER
ENCHANTING. PAPER-CUTTING IS AN
ANCIENT CRAFT, BUT IS STILL AS SIMPLE,
CHEAP AND SATISFYING AS EVER.

Jewelled hearts

These pretty little heart-shaped decorations are full of cultural references. The heart is a much-used folk art motif: Scandinavians – whose Christmas traditions influence our own so deeply – always have hearts on their trees. These shown here were inspired by Mexican tin hearts.

YOU WILL NEED... *Cardboard – off-cuts from picture mounts are ideal • Marker pen • Scalpel • Cutting mat or board • Coloured metallic wrapping paper (sweet wrappers would do) • Spray glue • Sharp scissors • High-tack bonding glue, such as UHU • Jewelled haberdashery trimmings • Gold and other colour fabric paints in tubes • Hole punch • Paperclips*

2 *Cut a rough rectangle of coloured metallic wrapping paper for each heart, and coat the backs of the papers with glue. Place the heart-shaped cardboard pieces in the centre of their papers.*

1 *Draw one heart, about 10 cm (4 in) long, on the cardboard with marker pen and cut it out with a scalpel, backed by a mat or board, or with sharp scissors. Use this as a template to draw out other hearts, as many as you wish, and cut these out, too.*

3 *Trim the paper with scissors to within one centimetre of the heart, then snip this border at intervals and mould it round the curves and stick it down on the back.*

4 Use the high-tack bonding glue to stick a selection of 'jewels' to the hearts, spacing them attractively and varying the patterns from heart to heart.

5 Use a tube of gold fabric paint to create dotted 'settings' for the jewels. The fabric paint in other colours can also be used on the hearts to create decorative patterns.

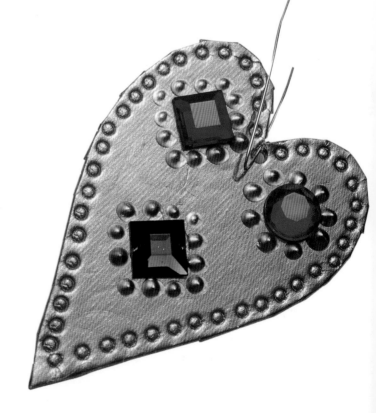

6 To use the hearts as tree decorations, first punch a hole in each at the centre top. Partly unwind metal paperclips and push them through the holes, and then hang them by loops onto the tree.

Paper chains

The paper chains and shelf fringe are both products of an old-fashioned paper-cutting art form. Stewart is a master lino and stencil cutter, but he is equally happy working with the many and versatile types of paper now available. He used glassine paper from an art shop, but other coloured papers can also be used, as long as they are both thin enough to fold and strong enough to hold their shape. Cut the paper into long strips – about 5 cm (2 in) wide. Fold each strip over and under to concertina it up into a wadge. Cut out shapes and holes in star and diamond shapes using sharp scissors, and use pinking shears to produce the zig-zag edges. Our pictures show the shapes the Waltons used, but you can design any pattern you like, practising first with short strips of paper. When you have finished cutting, pull the chains out of the concertina to produce the finished decorative strips: the most charming and low-cost decorations of all.

Shelf fringe

The concertina portions of the shelf fringe are about 12.5 x 20 cm (5 x 8 in) in size. Fold the paper strip and, leaving a plain border at the top edge where the decoration is to be attached to the shelf, cut a scalloped edge with pinking shears. Use a multi-sized

hole punch to cut out small, differently-shaped holes. The pattern here is copied from a Mexican decorative border, found in a book. Once cut, unfold the fringe and attach it to the shelf with small dots of Blu-Tack. In the evening, the fringe can cast wonderful shadows onto the wall behind.

Painted pine cones

Pine cones represent the earliest stage of Christmas decoration plans as they need to be gathered in autumn. Your first step, then, is a walk in a conifer forest in October to collect nature's free treasures. Once the cones have thoroughly dried out, they last forever and will not rot.

To make the 'stems' which will hold the pines upright or allow them to be hung from the tree, prise in a nail or a skewer to make a hole at the base of each cone, then push in a piece of florist's wire about 15 cm (6 in) long, using a blob of craft glue to secure it. Next, spray paint the cones gold or silver. When the paint is dry, brush coloured paints onto the tips to highlight the edges of the cones. Finally, brush the cones with PVA glue and dip them into a bowl of glitter – gold, silver or coloured.

THE BENDY STEMS ARE EASY TO FORM INTO LOOPS TO HANG THE CONES FROM THE TREE, WHERE THEY ALMOST LOOK AS IF THEY ARE GROWING NATURALLY. ALTERNATIVELY, YOU CAN USE THE CONES IN A VASE OR POT AS DECORATIONS IN THEIR OWN RIGHT, A COLLECTION OF WOODY SNOWFLAKE FORMATIONS.

The beauty of window stencils is that they look good from both inside and outside the house, where they make a definite Christmas statement. They cast wonderful shadows, which dance in the firelight.

Window Stencilling

YOU WILL NEED... *Paper • Pencil • Stencil card • Masking tape or low-tack spray adhesive • Scalpel • Cutting mat or board • Canvas shoe whitener • Stencil paints in red and yellow • Artist's medium-sized brush*

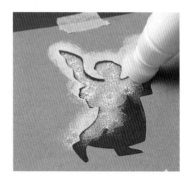

1 Draw an outline of an angel and another, larger outline of a star shape on paper with a pencil; or, you could use the outline of photocopies of an angel and star from a book or from a source-book of motifs. Attach the paper images to pieces of stencil card with masking tape or a low-tack spray adhesive.

2 Using the scalpel, and backed with a mat or board, cut round the lines of the images to make the stencils. Hold the scalpel at a slight angle, slanting inwards towards the cut-out middle, to give a bevelled edge, which will prevent smudging when you come to paint.

3 Attach the stencils to the window in position with masking tape. Paint on canvas shoe whitener to colour the angel, using the sponge applicator on the tube itself.

4 Carefully remove the stencil card, revealing the finished angel. The stencil can now be repositioned elsewhere on the window to paint another. Repeat the exercise to get the required overall effect.

WE USED EXACTLY THE SAME STENCILLING
METHOD TO PAINT DECORATIVE STARS,
BUT USED COLOURED STENCIL PAINTS
INSTEAD OF THE SHOE WHITENER. WE
CENTRED ONE STAR ON EACH PANE, AND
POSITIONED SIX ANGELS TO SWIRL AROUND
IT. THE VIEW THROUGH THE STENCILLED
WINDOW PANES FROM OUTSIDE IS BRIGHT
AND INVITING, WITH ALL THE COLOUR
AND WARMTH THAT CHARACTERISES THE
CHRISTMAS OF OUR IMAGINATIONS.

This is the part of the Christmas preparations which everyone seems to leave until a last, more time-consuming-than-you-thought rush. The whole problem is eased if you have a single wrapping plan in mind.

Cellophane Wrapping

The materials here are simple, cheap and easily available – newsprint, coloured or clear cellophane, adhesive tape (which becomes invisible on the cellophane) and ribbons. The trick which personalises the presents is to chose newsprint which suits the recipients – comics for the children, fanzines for teenagers, *Financial Times* pink for business brains, and so on.

Wrap presents in the newsprint, cover over with a second wrapping of cellophane, secure with adhesive tape, and then tie with ribbons. The Waltons have used an attractive combination of wide and thin ribbons, and created bows by looping the ribbons over and over and securing them at the centre with florist's wire.

Cut up brightly-coloured translucent plastic filing folders into parcel tag shapes. Fix round sticky labels onto an edge of the parcel tag and then punch

a hole through it with an ordinary hole-puncher. Write the greeting on with a spirit-based permanent marker pen, and attach the tags to the presents by threading through the metal ends of treasury tags.

BELOW: YOU MAY ALREADY HAVE TO HAND MANY OF THE MATERIALS NEEDED TO WRAP THE PRESENTS.
LEFT: THE COLOURFUL ABUNDANCE OF PAPER, BOWS, TAGS AND CELLOPHANE REFLECTS THE LIGHTS OF THE CHRISTMAS TREE AND DELIGHTS YOUNG ROXY WALTON.

KEVIN McCLOUD

A *Medieval* Feast

Gardening is a passion for
Kevin McCloud and his family
and, for them, following the ancient custom of bringing
winter foliage into the house adds life and magic.

The stone farmhouse in the Mendip Hills where the McCloud family lives dates back to the sixteenth century, and was built on the site of a medieval resting house on the Pilgrim Route to Glastonbury. From medieval times, people have brought evergreen foliage inside for Christmas – and, in earlier pagan times, for the winter solstice – and it carried far more complex meanings than the purely decorative. Red-berried holly was a powerful fertility symbol and would safeguard the house from goblins; seen as a full-blooded, masculine plant, it was complemented by sinuous, feminine ivy with her cool black berries. All evergreen plants, in leaf when others are dead, were seen as symbols of the continuity of life throughout the winter.

Plants are a cheap and green alternative to conventional Christmas decorations. Kevin makes the most of his rural setting by using all it provides. He combines his creative skills with his knowledge of nature to develop a foliage-based Christmas design scheme which celebrates tradition and echoes the folklore of ancient Britain.

RIGHT: SAM THE AIREDALE TERRIER
STANDS SENTRY IN THE DOORWAY, WITH
ITS ARCH OF HOLLY AND IVY. EXTENDING
DECORATIONS TO THE OUTSIDE ADDS A
WELCOMING TOUCH FOR VISITORS.

Shades of Green

At first glance, the holly and ivy round the farmhouse portico appear to be growing plants which have been there for decades.

The decoration around the doorway was put up quickly and surprisingly easily. Two sturdy branches of a sycamore tree that came down in the autumn, complete with lovely lichen-covered bark, are used for the 'trunks' either side. You can create a holly arch around most doorways. For his, Kevin banged nails into the walls at varying heights and then attached green wires to the 'trunks' and tied these around the nails. Branches of holly (any of the five varieties which can be found in the countryside) are in turn tied with wire onto the top of the trunks and occasionally secured against a nail. As few as four holly branches were needed. Long tendrils of ivy are then wound up the branches. Another clump of ivy is then shoved in to hide the obvious knot of branches and wire at the top of the trunks, as can be seen in the photographs below. At the apex of the foliage arch hangs a welcoming candle lantern.

Once they have passed through the outside door, visitors are caught by the mistletoe fixed above the inside arch. Mistletoe is an ancient symbol of fertility, with its white berries between parted leaves. We still believe in its aphrodisiac powers and claim our Christmas kissing rights. A single berry should be removed from the sprig for each kiss.

The Bedecked Chandelier

A chandelier decorated with nothing but ivies and a table laden with fruits fill the dining-room with Christmas spirit.

Kevin's dining-room has a magnificent antique chandelier with a jaunty gold tassel, but even if your light fittings and lamps aren't as glamorous you can still decorate them. The secret of success here is discipline, rather than excess. Too much ivy will smother the shape and simply look messy. Kevin took long strings of climbing ivy from plants covering the old walls in his garden to wind round the edges and between the loops of the chandelier candle-holders. Berried ivy was draped in bunches near the candles and above the tassel. He then tangled the ivy around the hanging chain and added a few bunches of bright red plastic cherries to give just a hint of lusciousness. Ivy is a sympathetic plant to hang above a Christmas feast: it was once thought that its black berries could counter the damaging effects of alcohol.

ABOVE: A FLEUR-DE-LIS WALL SCONCE IS LIGHTLY HUNG WITH BERRIED IVY, ECHOING THE DECORATIVE THEME AROUND THE ROOM. RIGHT: A DETAIL OF THE CHANDELIER SHOWS THE VARIEGATED LEAVES OF THE CLIMBING IVY AND THE BRIGHT, SHINY EVERGREEN OF THE BERRIED SECTION OF THE PLANT. BLACK BERRIES HANG JUST ABOVE THE DINERS' HEADS, LIKE A WORD OF WARNING.

THE TABLE DECORATIONS ARE STRAIGHT FROM NATURE, WHO PROVIDES ALL THE APPROPRIATE WINTER REDS AND GREENS: CRIMSON POMEGRANATES, THE VARIOUS GREEN HUES OF MELONS, ARTICHOKES, SHINY NEW COB NUTS AND FRESH FIGS. A BOWL IN THE CENTRE SPARKLES WITH GILDED NUTS. PEWTER JUGS AND BOWLS, POLYCHROMIC EARTHENWARE PLATES AND A BACKDROP OF CREWELWORK CURTAINS MAKE THIS CHRISTMAS SETTING LOOK CENTURIES OLD.

This tree is proof that you don't need fairy lights to provide sparkle. It is hung with gilded fruit, nuts and shells that reflect both the daylight and the electric or candle light of the evening.

Gilded Nature

The magic of a Christmas tree is in its glitter and glow, representing, particularly for children, all the excitement and anticipation of presents and games and a relaxation of normal domestic rules. Tinsel and lights begin to seem rather feeble when you see how much lavishness Kevin conjures up in decorating a simple spruce with nothing but gilded apples and pears, nuts and shells.

It is possible that our ancestors would have preserved apples and pears for Christmas, perhaps sealing them in airtight containers and burying them in the earth until winter. Certainly, wild pear trees and crab apples are recorded as having grown in Britain since Anglo-Saxon times. The apple tree, with its soft bark, is also one of the favourite host growing places of mistletoe.

Gilding the fruit, nuts and shells is not as difficult or expensive as you might imagine, as Kevin demonstrates overleaf. His gilded delights are not edible, although in theory, you could use just real 22ct gold leaf on the fruit and create edible snacks for the tree which would be far more enticing than hollow chocolate baubles. You'll need to cover the fruit in honey first to allow the gold leaf to stick.

LEFT: THE EARLY ENGLISH THEME OF KEVIN'S CHRISTMAS IS CONTINUED WITH THE 'MEDIEVAL' WRAPPING PAPERS FOR THE PRESENTS UNDER THE TREE, THE ECCLESIASTICAL CANDLESTICK AND THE BARE WOOD OF A STURDY COUNTRY TABLE.

Gilding fruit, nuts and shells

Metal leaf is very thin and delicate and can be difficult to handle. To help, Kevin advises that before touching the leaf, you dust your hands with talcum powder, so that the leaf will stick to the size on the fruit and nuts and not to you.

YOU WILL NEED... *Shells, Brazil nuts, walnuts, apples and pears • Hand drill • Red oxide car spraypaint primer • Wundasize or an equivalent water-based size • Artist's or decorating brush • Brass and aluminium leaf, available in transfer booklets or as loose sheets (Kevin used loose) • Soft cloth • Shellac • Jeweller's threading wire*

1 *Drill a small hole for hanging in an appropriate place in the shells and nuts. You might need to make two adjacent holes in order to thread a hanging wire through the nuts.*

2 *Wash and dry the shells thoroughly to make sure that they are clean of salt. Spray the fruit, nuts and shells with red oxide primer to give a sealed and stable base for the gilding. Allow to dry.*
NB *Red oxide is poisonous.*

3 *Paint the fruit, nuts and shells with a coat of size, using an artist's or decorator's brush. This provides the glue which the metal leaf will stick to. Brush the size out to as thin a coat as possible and leave to dry for 6–7 hours.*

  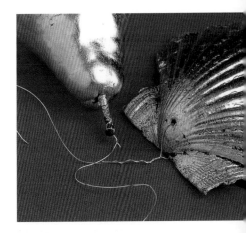

4 Tear pieces of the brass or aluminium leaf into manageable sizes and lay them over the surfaces of the fruit, nuts or shells. Rub gently with your fingertip to transfer the gilding, remove the paper backing and then polish with a soft cloth.

5 When all the pieces are gilded, brush over the top of the metal leaf with a thin coat of shellac, which will prevent the metal from tarnishing. The newly applied shellac will make the leaf look cloudy, but when it is dry the brilliance of the metal will shine back through.

6 Thread lengths of fine silver wire through the holes in the shells and nuts, and tie lengths of wire to the stalks of the apples and pears. Hang the finished decorations from the tree or wherever else they will enhance your decorations.

THE FINISHED CHEST IS SEEN IN ALL ITS RICH
SPLENDOUR. KEVIN USED AUTHENTIC MEDIEVAL COLOURS
– VERMILLION, ULTRAMARINE BLUE AND YELLOW OCHRE.

A *Treasure* Chest

Kevin is no exception in feeling that the most important element of Christmas is entertaining the children. This beautiful chest, like a massive medieval crown, is for their particular delight. Every year, the chest is brought out of hiding to be the centrepiece of their Christmas decorations; as the season progresses, it gradually fills up with presents for family and friends. On Christmas morning, its jewelled lid is finally heaved open to reveal the contents, and the gift-giving begins in earnest.

Some time and energy is needed to decorate the chest, which must be painted with care, *découpaged*, gilded and finally sealed over to ensure the patterns last. But, once made, a chest like this becomes an enviable family heirloom, a sort of treasure box in which years of children's excited anticipation is happily locked.

YOU WILL NEED... *Softwood or metal chest or trunk, either old or new • Medium-grade sandpaper • Emulsion paints in ultramarine, vermillion and yellow ochre • Selection of artist's or good soft decorating brushes • Scalpel • Cutting mat or board • Cardboard to make template • Shellac • Tape measure • Size • Brass leaf • Soft cloth • Decorative 'medieval' wrapping paper • Motifs of an angel and other scenes cut from old Christmas cards • PVA • Glue gun • Cabochon, half-circle glass 'jewels' or equivalent*

Decorating the chest

Kevin's special tip here is one for achieving perfect *découpage*. When applying PVA glue to the paper motifs, soak both sides of the paper with it, not just one. If you glue just the underside, the paper will curl up. If you soak both, and leave the paper for 3–4 minutes to expand in the glue, you will be able to apply the paper flat to the chest and watch it shrink back tightly, transforming it from simple wrapping paper into a magnificent medieval fresco.

1 *Sandpaper the box to remove splinters and to 'key' any spots of old paint and varnish. Kevin painted the sides of the chest and the top of the lid in blue and the sides of the lid in yellow ochre. Apply two or three coats of paint, drying and sanding down in between to achieve a really good finish, which is important for the later application of gilding and découpage. If your chest has trim mouldings, you could pick these out in vermillion paint. Artist's acrylic colours come in suitably intense, bright shades.*

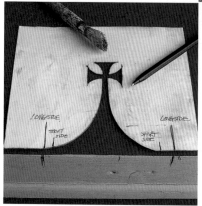

2 *Using a scalpel and working onto a cutting mat or board, cut a template from the cardboard, in the shape of the 'medieval' cross shown here, or in another pattern of your own devising. Paint the cut edges of the template with shellac to strengthen and waterproof them. Using a tape measure, find the central point of the top front edge of the lid of the chest, and paint on the first stencilled cross here in yellow ochre, adjoining the already painted yellow edge. Continue along the length of the edge of the lid; do the same on the other side and at the ends. Kevin used five crosses on each long side and two on each of the shorter sides.*

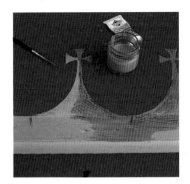

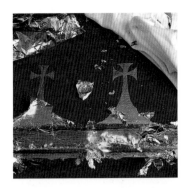

3 Paint size tinted with a small amount of any red emulsion or gouache paint onto the areas of the crosses with a brush. It is important to tint the size so that you can see where it has been applied and fill in any missing areas. It may help to place the stencil card back into position over the crosses so that you do not paint the size onto the blue background. Take time with this stage and don't be too slapdash.

4 Apply the gold-coloured brass leaf to the sized crosses, tracing their outline and pressing it on with your fingers. Peel away paper and rub off any excess leaf with a soft cloth. Apply a coat of shellac over the top of the gilded decoration with a brush, to seal it and prevent it from tarnishing. Try not to get the shellac onto the blue paint, as it may turn it a muddy shade.

5 Next, apply the découpage decoration. Cut the side panels from sheets of wrapping paper, together with strips of paper to go around the edge of the lid, under the crosses, and above the trim on the chest. Then cut an attractive angel motif from a Christmas card for the middle of the lid, and other scenes to go either side of the wrapping-paper panels. Stick the paper elements to the chest with a 50/50 solution of PVA and water, soaking the paper on both sides and applying the glue to the chest as well.

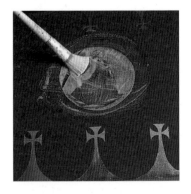

6 When the paste is dry, paint over the top of the découpaged patterns with more of the PVA solution to seal and varnish them.

7 Using a glue gun, stick on the cabochon 'jewels' between the crosses on the lid and along the lid edge, giving the top of the chest the appearance of a medieval crown. For an extra finish, line the inside of the box with decorative wrapping paper, sticking it on with more of the PVA solution (or with wallpaper paste).

Acknowledgements

The designers, author and publishers would like to thank the following for their help in the preparation of this book:

Victoria Gibbs, Samantha Kay, Ana-Paula Lloyd, Charlotte Lochhead, Rachel Matthews, Eleanor Preston-Gill, Inga Schulze.

Richard Mabey's book *Flora Britannica* (Sinclair-Stevenson, 1996) informed our understanding of the history and folklore of winter foliage.

Useful Addresses

Sheets of motifs suitable for print room arrangements (page 14)
The National Trust Shop
Blewcoat School
23 Caxton Street, London SW1H 0PY
Tel: 0171 222 2877
Mail order tel: 01225 790800

Fake flowers (page 28)
Borovick Fabrics Ltd
16 Berwick Street, London W1V 4HP
Tel: 0171 437 2180

Mexican crafts and decorations (page 36)
Mexique
67 Sheen Lane, London SW14 8AD
Tel: 0181 392 2345

Gilding kits (page 58)
Pear Tree Crafts
Pear Tree Cottage, Wanstow
Nr. Shepton Mallet, Somerset BA4 4TF
Tel: 01749 850 886

Wrapping papers (page 61)
Paperchase
213 Tottenham Court Road
London W1P 9AF
Tel: 0171 580 8496
(and other various branches)
Mail order available

Chests and trunks (page 61)
Try school suppliers in your area.